MW01101633

SELF-MANAGING
TEAMS

Better Management Skills

This highly popular range of inexpensive paperbacks covers all areas of basic management. Practical, easy to read and instantly accessible, these guides will help managers to improve their business or communication skills. Those marked * are available on audio cassette.

The books in this series can be tailored to specific company requirements. For further details, please contact the publisher, Kogan Page, telephone 0171 278 0433, fax 0171 837 6348.

Be a Successful Supervisor
Business Etiquette
Coaching Your Employees
Creative Decision-making
Creative Thinking in Business
Delegating for Results
Effective Meeting Skills
Effective Performance Appraisals*
Effective Presentation Skills
Empowerment
First Time Supervisor
Get Organised!
Goals and Goal Setting
How to Communicate
　Effectively*
How to Develop a Positive
　Attitude*
How to Develop Assertiveness
How to Motivate People*
How to Understand Financial
　Statements
How to Write a Staff Manual
Improving Employee Performance
Improving Relations at Work
Keeping Customers for Life
Leadership Skills for Women

Learning to Lead
Make Every Minute Count*
Managing Disagreement
　Constructively
Managing Organisational Change
Managing Part-Time Employees
Managing Quality Customer
　Service
Managing Your Boss
Marketing for Success
Memory Skills in Business
Mentoring
Office Management
Productive Planning
Project Management
Quality Customer Service
Rate Your Skills as a Manager
Sales Training Basics
Selling Professionally
Successful Negotiation
Successful Telephone Techniques
Systematic Problem-solving and
　Decision-making
Team Building
Training Methods that Work
The Woman Manager

SELF-MANAGING TEAMS

Robert F Hicks and Diane Bone

KOGAN
PAGE

Copyright © Crisp Publications Inc 1990

All rights reserved. No part of this book may be
reproduced or transmitted in any form or by any
means now known or to be invented, electronic or
mechanical, including photocopying, recording, or
by any information storage or retrieval system, without
written permission from the author or publisher,
except for the brief inclusion of quotations in a review.

First published in the United States of America
in 1990 by Crisp Publications Inc, 95 First Street,
Los Altos, California 94022, USA.

This edition first published in Great Britain in
1991 by Kogan Page Ltd, 120 Pentonville Road,
London N1 9JN. Reprinted 1995.

British Library Cataloguing in Publication Data

A CIP record for this book is available from the British Library.

ISBN 0–7494–0527–9

Typeset by DP Photosetting, Aylesbury, Bucks
Printed and bound in Great Britain by
Clays, St Ives plc

Contents

About This Book

Self-managing Teams is not like most books. It stands out from other self-help books in an important way. It's not a book to read – it's a book to *use*. The unique format and many work sheets encourage the reader to apply directly what is learned.

The objective of *Self-managing Teams* is to explain what SMTs are, and show the benefits they can bring to an organisation. This book teaches you how to establish and maintain an SMT programme.

Self-managing Teams (and other titles in this series) can be used effectively in a number of ways. Here are some possibilities:

- *Individual study.* Because the book is self-instructional, all that is needed is a quiet place, some time and a pencil.

- *Workshops and seminars.* This book is very useful as the missing document for any organisation wishing to set up a self-managing team programme.

- *Open learning.* Books can be used by those unable to attend head office training sessions.

There are several other possibilities that depend on the objectives, induction programme or ideas of the user.

One thing is certain: even after it has been read, this book will be looked at – and thought about – again and again.

Preface

Is your organisation looking for new ways to improve productivity? Is your company culture ready for a change? Does your work life 'wish list' look anything like this?

I would like my organisation to allow me to:

- Accept more responsibility
- Gain more autonomy
- Share a sense of accomplishment with others
- Learn new skills
- Gain greater rewards for what I do.

Self-managing teams may be the answer to making the changes you want. For several years forward-looking organisations that have experimented with self-managing teams (SMTs), have experienced increases in quality and productivity of up to 30 per cent.

SMTs are small, autonomous work groups, often called 'business teams' or 'self-directed work groups' that contract with higher management to take complete responsibility for a product, project or service. Team members perform their own jobs and 'cross train' team-mates as well. SMTs also take on varying degrees of management responsibility. These may include planning, scheduling, ordering, hiring, evaluating or setting quality standards.

Whether you are a manager who wants to give employees more autonomy, a member of a functioning SMT looking for helpful hints, a task force member seeking to help yourself or your colleagues to be more effective, or a human resource development professional interested in SMT training requirements, this book will help you to find answers, get your SMT off to a good start, and keep it running smoothly. It addresses such questions as:

What are self-managing teams (SMTs) and how did they evolve?
Do managers have a place in SMTs?
What are the critical success factors?
Should your group become a self-managing team?
How do you contract for an SMT?
What are the benefits?
How do you correct problems?
What kind of training do you need?

Although SMTs aren't for every organistion, they may be right for you. If you are flexible, willing to work, and value positive change, read on. We encourage you to explore a strategy that holds enormous potential for improving both productivity and employee satisfaction.

PART 1
Preparation

CHAPTER 1
What is a Self-managing Team?

A self-managing team (SMT) is a work group that operates with varying degrees of autonomy and without a visible manager. It assumes management responsibility in addition to performing its specific jobs. These responsibilities may include planning, organising, directing and monitoring both their jobs and the administrative functions that support them. The team learns and shares jobs usually performed by a manager. In a fully functioning SMT, control comes from within the group, rather than from outside it.

Review the jobs listed below and see which you already perform as part of your current work assignment. Tick any you would like to assume and/or share with your work group. In considering these jobs, you are beginning to evaluate yourself as a potential SMT member. I would like to:

- [ ] Run weekly schedule meetings
- [ ] Identify goals
- [ ] Persuade others to adopt goals
- [ ] Schedule and coordinate group and individual tasks
- [ ] Learn colleagues' jobs as part of cross-training
- [ ] Develop a training plan
- [ ] Set standards
- [ ] Take on new staff or make recruitment recommendations
- [ ] Screen applicants and interview job candidates

☐ Provide induction for new team members

☐ Train and provide career guidance

☐ Evaluate new team members during their probationary period

☐ Plan and adopt a budget

☐ Review performance data

☐ Meet requests from inside and outside the team

☐ Solve problems by team consensus.

Where are the managers?

Even though SMTs are, by definition, self-managing, all SMTs report to *someone*. Managers are visible in varying degrees, depending on the origin and purpose of the SMT. Some typical management situations for an SMT include the following:

- Team reports in a 'skip-level' pattern, reporting to managers two or more levels above them. These managers act as integrators/facilitators.
- Team reports to 'absentee' manager away on extended special assignment, and members function independently while the manager is absent.
- Team becomes self-managing because its manager has broad responsibility for managing several functions, so is seldom present.
- Team becomes self-managing when a top level manager eliminates layers of management and instructs a team to report directly to him or her but requests that they manage their own function.
- Team becomes self-managing when its manager leaves the organisation, and the work group is given, and accepts, the opportunity to self-manage. In this case, a sponsor or contract manager is chosen (usually by the team) to provide guidance through organisational minefields.

- Team consists of 'cross disciplines' that don't fit into traditional management structures (engineers, production control, programmers). They can't find a 'manager' so they usually report to higher management responsible for a 'product'.

When does a team become self-managing?

Teams may operate on a self-management scale, with some more autonomous than others. The chart below shows how and when a team becomes self-managing.

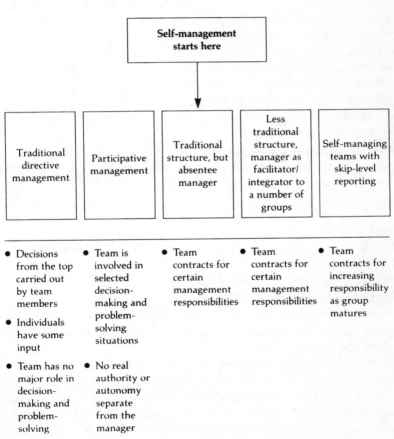

		Self-management starts here		
Traditional directive management	Participative management	Traditional structure, but absentee manager	Less traditional structure, manager as facilitator/ integrator to a number of groups	Self-managing teams with skip-level reporting
• Decisions from the top carried out by team members • Individuals have some input • Team has no major role in decision-making and problem-solving	• Team is involved in selected decision-making and problem-solving situations • No real authority or autonomy separate from the manager	• Team contracts for certain management responsibilities	• Team contracts for certain management responsibilities	• Team contracts for increasing responsibility as group matures

Why are self-managing teams important?

New technology. Staff reduction. Profit sharing. Today, organisations are looking for responsible ways to lower costs and increase productivity. To survive, they are becoming more innovative, especially in finding creative ways to use their employees' talents.

Employees are an organisation's greatest resource

Increasingly, organisations are giving employees more ownership and autonomy. They find that employees work harder and need less hand holding when they have more control of their jobs and more freedom to choose how they will do them. Recent statistics indicate that organisations that encourage employee involvement are increasing productivity by 30 per cent and more. Workers who participate in self-directed work groups (self-managing teams) report higher motivation, increased self-worth, and greater pride in their work.

SMTs 'self-correct' quickly

Forward-looking organisations emphasise quality and excellence. They need skilled people who can perform several tasks and respond quickly to change. SMT members are trained to 'self-correct'. In other words, they identify problems and correct them quickly. As organisations eliminate layers of management and staff to increase cost effectiveness and improve communication, SMTs are replacing managers by doing the job themselves.

SMTs provide today's work force with a means of self-expression

Intelligent people want psychological enrichment and control of their lives. One common complaint among employees is that they are frustrated in achieving organisational needs, because management erects too many barriers. SMTs provide opportunities for people to put their cards on the table and take responsibility for their actions. They are a logical way to group people who want to remain in an organisation but value working creatively. As organisations struggle with the problem of too few people in the work force, SMTs are serving as training grounds for learning multiple tasks.

How did SMTs originate?

SMTs have evolved from the concept of the quality circle. As quality circle offspring they have 'grown up' and embarked on lives of their own. In quality circles employees analyse and solve organisational problems. Employees are well trained in teamwork and problem-solving, but they have little power beyond calling attention to problems and making suggestions for change.

SMTs go far beyond quality circles. As part of an SMT, employees are trained to use their skills daily to schedule, assign tasks, coordinate with other groups (and sometimes customers and suppliers), set goals, evaluate performance and address discipline issues. Project management and participative management are SMT cousins, as each emphasises sharing tasks and teamwork.

Should your work group become an SMT?

Perhaps you are already on your way to becoming an SMT. To gauge how prepared your group is to take the next step, tick those statements below that apply to your work group now.

☐ Our manager wants us to take more responsibility.

☐ We share common goals.

☐ We are ready to learn new skills.

☐ We work well as a group.

☐ We like each other.

☐ We communicate effectively.

☐ We communicate effectively with people outside the team.

☐ We are good at articulating our expectations.

☐ Our organisation is creative and welcomes new ideas.

☐ We are not afraid of hard work.

☐ We believe that setting goals is important.

☐ We don't worry about what other people think (SMTs are not popular with everyone).

☐ We have determination.

☐ We are willing to negotiate solutions to problems.

☐ We are comfortable sharing rewards and receiving recognition as a team.

☐ We thank each other for help.

☐ We can identify and solve problems quickly.

☐ We can solve disruptive behaviour and accept discipline.

☐ We are willing to do more than our share when necessary.

☐ We have an upper-level manager who will support us.

The more items you ticked, the better your group's chance of becoming a successful SMT.

Review

1. Based on the information in this chapter, write your description of an SMT on the lines below.

_____

_____

_____

_____

_____

_____

2. What is your current management situation?

_____

_____

_____

_____

_____

_____

_____

3. How close is your team to becoming self-managing?

_____

_____

_____

_____

_____

_____

_____

CHAPTER 2

Is Your Organisation Ready for Self-managing Teams?

Some organisations are perfect candidates for SMTs. They have a supportive culture (environment) and their management welcomes constructive change. Corporate officers and top managers determine company culture and evolution. A company culture – the totality of its environment, social norms and management behaviour – is top management's expression of itself.

Here are two examples of workers and their environments for you to read and assess. Circle the description you consider most appropriate in each case.

Paul works for Accountware Co. He designs computer software for accounting firms. His company is located in an old part of town in a run-down red brick building. The office where he works is devoid of pictures or plants because the management frowns on personalising work space. Paul needs new equipment but must complete so much paperwork to make a request that he can't find the time to requisition it. Everyone in the company comes early and stays late because deadlines are frequent and unyielding. How would you describe Paul's work culture?

Open   Friendly   Innovative   Flexible   Dismal

Sue, a medical technologist, has re-entered the work force after taking time off to have a child. She has good skills, but they are somewhat outdated because medical technology advances so rapidly. The General Hospital, where she is employed, is providing Sue with a complete analysis of her current skill level, appropriate classes to upgrade required skills for her job, and supervised training on the job when classes are unavailable. The management is supportive and helpful when Sue needs information or requests assistance. Sue is relearning her job quickly and hopes to be working at full capacity within three months. How would you describe Sue's work culture?

Open   Friendly   Innovative   Flexible   Dismal

How would you describe your work culture?

_____

_____

_____

_____

Organisation checklist

Listed below are characteristics of organisational cultures that would be likely to support SMTs. Tick those that you believe describe your organisation. If you can tick 12 or more, your group has a good chance of developing a successful SMT that will be supported by your company culture.

Your organisation:

☐ Promotes cooperative relationships over competitive ones

☐ Sets high standards for all functions

- [ ] Pays fair wages
- [ ] Recognises individual contributions
- [ ] Encourages individual accountability and responsibility
- [ ] Seldom interferes when work is progressing as planned
- [ ] Respects the time needed to complete a process
- [ ] Embraces the 'WAITT' philosophy (We're All In This Together)
- [ ] Pays attention to employees' interpersonal requirements (security, good working conditions, training, social needs)
- [ ] Believes that 'playing safe' is not always advisable
- [ ] Has short- and long-term goals
- [ ] Is people-orientated
- [ ] Has a positive vision of the future
- [ ] Believes in its products and service
- [ ] Supports the community
- [ ] Is willing to try new ideas.

You be the judge

UK Company Ltd has indicated to its employees that it is interested in their response to the concept of SMTs. The SMTs would be voluntary and self-initiated by interested teams. Management would support interested teams in establishing goals and getting started. Five different groups of colleagues who have similar work tasks have come together to discuss SMTs. Based on the statements below, which groups are good candidates for succeeding as an SMT?

Group 1
'We like our manager, and we like being managed. Our manager tells us exactly what to do, and we don't have to think for

ourselves. We hope things won't change because we like them the way they are.'

Yes ☐   No ☐

Group 2
'We like UK Company but find that management often blocks our productivity with too many controls. We would like more responsibility and autonomy in our work.'

Yes ☐   No ☐

Group 3
'Our group is very creative and is always coming up with new ideas. We would like to try some of our ideas, because we think they will improve productivity. We're willing to take responsibility for implementing them. If we fail (we don't believe we will), we will accept responsibility for that, as well.'

Yes ☐   No ☐

Group 4
'We are very independent thinkers. We like working alone, with little interference from anyone. We realise teamwork is important but, to be honest, we communicate only when necessary. We're happy to stay out of the limelight and do our work without a lot of fuss.'

Yes ☐   No ☐

Group 5
'Everyone in our group has been employed at UK Company for a long time. Lately we've felt the need for a challenge. Our organisation isn't promoting people the way it used to, so we haven't had a chance to become managers. We need stimulation. Perhaps learning new job skills and gaining some management techniques would help us to rebuild pride in our work.

Yes ☐   No ☐

Author response

Authors' comments. Groups 1 and 4 are not candidates for SMTs. They either like working for a manager, or they prefer to work alone. They are also resistant to change. Groups 2, 3 and 5 are good candidates. They would like more autonomy, aren't afraid of the possibility of failure, and are ready for a change.

Review

1. Is your organisation ready for SMTs?

    _____

    _____

    _____

    _____

2. Why or why not?

    _____

    _____

    _____

    _____

3. If your organisation is ready, what are its major strengths? If not, what factors would prevent SMTs from flourishing?

    _____

    _____

    _____

    _____

CHAPTER 3

Is Your Management Ready for Self-managing Teams?

This chapter will help employees to evaluate available management support for SMTs and instruct managers how they can best support them. Management support for SMTs is a critical success factor. Without it, any scheme involving SMTs will fail. Support means that management recognises the need for SMTs and values their contributions. Support also means that management is willing to support SMTs (without interfering) and is committed to helping them succeed.

Your organisation's business goals must be in line with SMT functions because SMTs are created to help organisations achieve their goals. One company might have a corporate goal of increasing its flexibility and responding faster to customers' needs. This goal is both a legitimate business need and a realistic expectation for an SMT. The business goal of another company might be to use its internal resources more efficiently. Because SMTs often employ cross-training as a means of increasing employee effectiveness, an SMT could be a vehicle for achieving this goal. In all situations where management is considering SMTs, *an explicit connection* must exist between the goals of the organisation and the establishment of SMTs.

> You must have management support to succeed!

Beginning on page 30 is a list of management contributions to help your SMT to get started and to grow. On the lines following each item, write your personal or team assessment of your management's stand on each issue. If you are a manager, assess your ability to provide these items. If you think you may not receive (or be able to give) this support, use your problem-solving skills to suggest alternatives. If you must search for alternatives under *every* item, you are *not* ready to establish self-managing teams.

Requirements for management support

1. Set clear goals

Management's greatest contribution to any SMT is to establish clear goals and expectations. Management must share goals openly and freely with team members. *These goals must be expressed in writing.* A written agreement should set out all expectations relating to establishment, operating procedure, ground rules, salary administration, incentives, etc. A written agreement provides a means of clarifying those areas where agreement is critical to success.

Your assessment: _____

_____

_____

Alternatives: _____

_____

_____

_____

2. Show willingness

Willingness is an action item. Management must demonstrate that it is willing to support SMTs by its actions – not just its words. Management expresses willingness by helping to establish the SMT, granting the level of autonomy for which the team is ready, and when there is no manager, finding a sponsor. A sponsor is a person with clout who supports the team and 'runs interference' when the team experiences problems.

Your assessment: _____

_____

_____

Possible names of sponsors: His/Her willingness:

_____   _____

_____   _____

_____   _____

Alternatives:

_____

_____

3. Provide protection from political fallout

SMTs push power further down in the organisational hierarchy, which may threaten existing power bases. People may feel they are losing decision-making power. This perceived threat may cause political obstacles and blocks. Sponsors help to protect SMTs from political hailstorms, so they must have enough political awareness, skill and power to play the role.

Your assessment: _____

_____

_____

Alternatives: _____

_____

_____

4. Acquire resources

New SMTs may need more resources than normal to do their jobs. Such resources could include additional training, consulting services, equipment, part-time support staff, etc. Sponsors with management authority can be invaluable in securing extra resources.

Your assessment: _____

_____

_____

_____

Alternatives: _____

_____

_____

_____

5. Give feedback

Any functioning unit needs feedback, particularly with a new process. Sponsors need to serve as reliable, consistent sources of input relative to the performance and progress of the SMT *from management's point of view*. This feedback helps the SMT to self-correct as it proceeds.

Your assessment: _____

_____

_____

Alternatives: _____

_____

_____

6. Allow process time

SMTs have many process requirements and so considerable time may be required to show results. A sponsor can ease the pressure of expectations by displaying patience and a 'steady as she goes' attitude. SMT members must establish procedures for completing tasks, handling administrative functions, and working together effectively. They even need to adjust to making their own decisions (and accepting the consequences). Management must respect the process without necessarily expecting immediate results. Every SMT must go through a learning curve. Some groups will have longer learning curves than others.

Your assessment: _____

_____

_____

_____

_____

Alternative: _____

_____

_____

_____

_____

Now that you have looked at the management requirements, take a moment to assess your conclusions. If you can say 'Yes' to all the following questions, by all means move ahead with your proposal for your SMT.

	Yes	No	
1.	☐	☐	Does a clear business reason exist for adopting an SMT format?
2.	☐	☐	Is your management already participative?
3.	☐	☐	Does management understand what its role would be in leading and supporting an SMT?
4.	☐	☐	Has enough time been allotted to plan and organise your SMT?
5.	☐	☐	Are incentives in place to make an SMT personally worthwhile?
5.	☐	☐	Is the political climate in your organisation conducive to SMTs?

Guidelines for management

The process of forming an SMT is very fragile. To ensure success, management must support the team through its infancy and refrain from interfering until it is healthy enough to survive on its own. The following guidelines will help managers to make informed decisions on who should be involved, how to proceed, and what to expect. Tick those guidelines upon which you have already acted and number the others in the order in which you intend to implement them.

1. ☐ Select for success

You can maximise the probability of success in establishing your SMTs by selecting 'leading parts' candidates. The leading parts of an organisation are those work teams who are the most ready to engage in the SMT process. 'Leading parts' candidates possess some, or all, of the following characteristics:

- They already work well together.
- They have shown an interest in SMTs.
- They require low management maintenance.
- They have positive, forward-looking attitudes.
- They are willing to be test cases and to pilot an SMT project.

2. ☐ Create successful experiences

You will want your new SMT to perceive its change process in a positive light. When it does, it will be eager to take the next steps. You also want your colleagues and management to see the value of the new SMT. Therefore, you want to build in, document, and communicate successes in the beginning while you build the critical mass of support necessary for others to invest further energy in your project. Plan your SMT to create early success. Word-of-mouth feedback to the organisation is very powerful. The news of success travels fast and goes a long way towards gaining acceptance of the SMT adventure.

3. ☐ Go slow to go fast

Don't bite off more than you can chew. Be sure that resources, commitment and time are available to get your SMT off to a good start. Don't expect visible results prematurely. Creating an SMT is like building a foundation for a building. It must be done properly or it may crumble later on. So go slow, do it well, and the team will move faster as a result.

4. ☐ Put it in writing

Agreement between management and a new SMT must be expressed in writing. A written agreement should set out your expectations. What are your reasons for forming an SMT? What procedures will you use? (This step is especially important if your group will function at variance with traditional company procedures.) What are the ground rules for performance appraisals, salary administration, incentives, etc? A written agreement is a means of clarifying areas where agreement is imperative between management and the SMT.

5. ☐ Build in short *and* long-term goals

SMTs might drastically improve productivity in the short term, but they will suffer (or disintegrate) without long-term goals such as an improved work climate and opportunity for professional growth. Stressing both short- and long-term goals early avoids problems when the initial 'honeymoon' period is over or when the burst of early creativity ends.

Review

1. What is your overall assessment of your management's readiness to assist your SMT?

_____

_____

_____

_____

_____

_____

_____

2. As a manager, how would you assess your readiness to assist an SMT in your organisation?

_____

_____

_____

_____

_____

_____

CHAPTER 4
Are You and Your Team Ready for Self Managing?

What can an SMT provide for you and your team? Are you an employee about to change responsibilities, and are you eager to learn if a position in an SMT offers the challenge you need to make your work more exciting? Or has your manager suggested that your group become an SMT while he or she joins a special task force during the coming year? For which of the reasons listed below might you and your team consider an SMT? Tick those that apply to you.

☐ To learn more than one job (cross-training)

☐ To become involved in decision-making

☐ To gain greater financial rewards through skill-based pay and profit sharing

☐ To work in an atmosphere of group trust and respect

☐ To learn management skills

☐ To minimise interference from management

☐ To learn better self-accountability

☐ To achieve greater flexibility and faster response time

☐ To have more access to customers

☐ To increase self-esteem

☐ To become self-motivated

☐   To increase the desire to be at work

☐   To learn people skills

☐   To use time more effectively

☐   To learn how politics work.

Others (add your own):

☐

☐

☐

☐

What skills do you need?

As you read the following descriptions, see if you can identify which skill(s) these team members should develop in order to be more effective SMT members. List those from the previous page that you think apply. Note the authors' comments at the end of the exercise.

1. Sandy has recently joined an SMT at her company. She is having difficulty finding time to attend its weekly meetings because her customers phone unexpectedly. The telephone interrupts her constantly during meetings with other team members. Sandy has been late to meetings with team members several times because she is unable to find copies of agenda items in her overcrowded files. She often feels overwhelmed by her new responsibilities as an SMT member and is not sure if she has made the right decision by joining.

What training does Sandy need?

_____

_____

_____

2. Richard has been a member of an SMT for two years. He is enthusiastic about his group's project and enjoys the challenge of self-management. Recently, he was assigned to be a liaison (boundary manager) between his SMT and other departments. He must let departments know what his team is doing and how it can help other departments. He also talks to suppliers and customers regularly, keeping them informed of his team's needs and services. At times, he is not sure who to talk to and how to co-ordinate so much activity with so many people.

What training does Richard need?

_____

_____

_____

3. Thelma was uncertain about joining an SMT because she is shy. She did join, because she likes to be part of a group, but she says very little. When asked her opinion, she would express agreement with the majority of the team, but she seldom offered her own opinion. Although she undertook her assigned tasks willingly, she was reluctant to take her turn as team leader, for she was uncomfortable at making decisions and asking people to do things. People like Thelma but they wish she would speak her own mind more often.

What training does Thelma need?

_____

_____

_____

Authors' comments

1. Sandy is having trouble managing her time. She needs to set priorities and stick to them. She should attend a time management seminar to learn how to organise her work and handle multiple tasks.

2. Richard is ready for a seminar in boundary management. He is assigned to manage the external affairs of his SMT, and he needs to learn how to identify and co-ordinate the boundaries of his team and other groups. Then he can identify mutual issues and help to solve mutual problems.

3. Thelma needs to be more assertive and improve her ability to communicate. She is a good listener, but she must learn to express her ideas with confidence and authority.

SMTs thrive when people communicate effectively.

Case studies

Which of the following groups are good candidates for becoming an SMT? Use the guidelines from the preceding page to help you make your decision. Tick the 'Yes' or 'No' box at the end of the paragraph, and list your reasons in the blank space below. See the authors' comments on the opposite page.

Case 1

Sally, Manuel and Kate have been working in the same department of the bank for two years. They have related jobs, but each performs some specific tasks not related to what the others do. They are all eager to learn new skills and they attend an evening class on business management together. Their manager, Bob, is very supportive, but he is being promoted. A new manager has not been designated. The three have discussed many ways they can help their customers more quickly and efficiently and together they were awarded a plaque for 'The Best

Idea of the Month'. Before their manager leaves, they plan to talk to him about becoming an SMT.

☐ Yes ☐ No

Authors' comments

Sallie, Manuel, and Kate are good candidates for an SMT. They share the same interests and are motivated in their jobs. Before he leaves, their current manager can help them to set goals and write a contract assigning various responsibilities. This potential team is sufficiently strong and motivated to handle a transition to SMT status and the extra work involved in starting an SMT. They are mature enough to work out problems as they arise.

Case 2

Twenty employees of High Tech Ltd have been working on a long and complicated project directed by an autocratic manager. The employees, who are independent, creative thinkers, are fed up with the manager's authoritarian manner and have finally registered a complaint with one of the company directors. They have requested that they be allowed to become a self-managing team, so they can work more independently. The group feel they can get more done on their own than with a hard-nosed manager breathing down their necks.

☐ Yes ☐ No

Authors' comments

This group will have problems developing into an SMT. The group is too large to develop easily into a cohesive working unit. The group has been working in a tightly controlled environment and lacked an opportunity to practise team-building, problem-solving and negotiating skills. They are also independent thinkers, and although creativity has value, they must have a strong desire to work together in a cooperative manner. Their creativity may cause them to avoid more mundane management tasks such as scheduling and paperwork. Since they have followed the goals only of their manager they would need to identify their own goals and ensure they would be working towards the same ends. The length of their project may be too great for a new SMT to complete. The chances of their building a strong, committed team are remote.

Case 3

Frank Jason is the managing director of Frank and Sons Construction Company. Frank is innovative in his approach to employee development and involvement. He constantly looks for new ways to eliminate waste, reduce redundancy and increase productivity. His employees have been conducting quality circles for several years with good results. In weekly meetings, he shares his dreams and goals with his managers and supervisors and asks for their input. Recently, Jerry Billings, one of the supervisors, said that he wished to leave his supervisory position to run the heavy equipment on his project. He suggested that his group become an SMT. Jerry is willing to act as the first designated team leader to teach his colleagues how to do the supervisory job. Frank is considering the suggestion and exploring the possibility of an SMT for Jerry's work team.

☐ Yes ☐ No

Authors' comments

As Frank is managing director and supports teamwork, SMTs have a good chance of working in his organisation. Much of the work is organised around projects in a construction firm, so goals are easy to identify. Employees are already accustomed to giving input, and they understand the organisation's goals. They know that Frank would share business information with them to help them learn how to work together and with their suppliers and customers. This group has an excellent chance of becoming an SMT.

Review

1. Do you feel you are ready to join an SMT?

_____

_____

_____

_____

_____

_____

2. In which areas are you best qualified?

_____

_____

_____

_____

_____

3. In which areas do you need to improve?

_____

_____

_____

_____

_____

_____

_____

CHAPTER 5

Self-managing Teams – Facts and Fables

As you plan your SMT, be alert for potential obstacles to your success. Expectations based on idealised wishes can burst your balloon quickly when you face the reality (and hard work) of creating and supporting a dynamic, integrated team. Listed below are some expectations of SMTs. In your opinion, do these expectations usually occur as planned in SMTs? Are they facts or fables? Write 'True' next to those you believe to be true and 'False' next to those you believe are unrealistic. See the authors' comments at the end of the exercise.

1. I will have more autonomy without a supervising manager.
   _____

2. I will have more time for my own work without a manager's influence. _____

3. I will be able to do the job they pay me for and avoid irrelevant issues. _____

4. Working without a supervising manager will make my job easier. _____

If you answered 'False' for each of the expectations listed above, you are correct. The following explanations will help you to clarify your expectations and keep you grounded in reality.

1. In one sense, you *do* have more autonomy. You won't have a

manager looking over your shoulder. But instead, your team members will be looking over *both* shoulders. For your SMT to be successful, everyone on the team will have to be more involved in each other's work. The team works together to plan, co-ordinate, exchange information, and follow up. You may experience tremendous peer pressure, forcing you to live up to your commitments. Peer pressure reduces the feeling of absolute autonomy, but it is an essential part of your team's productivity.

2. First the bad news. Time pressure will not decrease. In fact, it may increase. For you, this may mean *more meetings.* Your group will represent itself at meetings that a manager normally attends. You and your team need a high degree of communication and co-ordination among yourselves and with others. Successful SMTs develop aggressive checking systems (including meetings) to be sure that work is being done properly and on time.

   Now the good news. The meetings you attend will be more meaningful and productive, because they are relevant and you are involved in the decisions. You 'count' in an SMT!

3. Few issues will be irrelevant. You will need to develop a much broader outlook. You will be interacting more directly with other organisational units and you will have to take their concerns into consideration when you make decisions. You will have to think of organisational issues, operational issues and political issues. How do your team's actions and decisions affect other organisational units? You will have to think long term.

> Proposal to management: 'Our commitment is to long-term success. We understand that short-term thinking produces long-term consequences. We will build bridges so we will not be at the mercy of the next day, the next product or the next administrator.'

4. Working without a manager will place additional responsibil-

ities on you. Managerial and supervisory duties will have to be distributed among team members. These will demand additional time and energy. During the start-up phase, you will be working on details of transition between your traditional role and your new role(s). For a while, you will be in a 'parallel process', establishing new ground rules and procedures *and* performing the day-to-day tasks you were employed to do.

Unrealised expectations are derived from *unrealistic* expectations. Unrealistic expectations slow the development of SMTs and demoralise the team. You must know what you are getting into.

Take time to share your perceptions on SMTs with other team members. List them below in the Review, then do a 'reality check' with people already in SMTs. Consider the information provided in this book. A realistic attitude will keep your team healthy and enthusiastic.

Review

1. What are your perceptions of SMTs?

_____

_____

_____

_____

_____

2. How are they different from what you have read in this book?

_____

_____

_____

_____

_____

3. What sources of information does your organisation have for
   learning about SMTs?

   _____

   _____

   _____

   _____

   _____

   _____

   _____

   _____

   _____

CHAPTER 6
The Change Machine

Imagine that you have a mysterious machine in the reception area of your office building. Everyone just calls it the 'change machine'. Anything you put into it comes out changed. Straight chairs come out with curves, ideas come out with new twists, travel vouchers switch you from Qantas to British Airways. Everyone uses the change machine, because your organisation values different ways of seeing things, doing things and adjusting to surprises. The change machine is a prototype of what happens in the world of business.

Your team decides to put all its plans for an SMT into the machine to gain insight into dealing with the changes you are making. You put into the change machine all your expectations and plans (even the rough draft of your proposal to management), and then you wait. The machine shakes and quivers then, suddenly, a large scroll pops out of the top. You unroll the scroll carefully. At the top is the title, 'Wise words about change'. The secrets of the change machine are in your hands. The machine has magnanimously performed to prepare you for your new adventure. Eagerly, you read on. The scroll begins . . .

Change is both toxic and tonic
As you plan your SMT, you are thrilled by the possibilities and the excitement of 'newness'. You will feel stimulated by the prospects of change. At the same time, you will also experience fear and uncertainty, even loss. You will feel exhilaration and anxiety, and sometimes you won't know which is which.

Change requires exchange

You are required to give up something old for something new. You must unlearn and relearn. You exchange a subordinate role for increased power and status. You exchange old values for new values. You will be giving up your cushion (your manager) for greater personal visibility. You must fully perceive the costs involved and, above all, you must firmly believe that what you are gaining is worth what you are giving up.

Change is stressless only for the mindless

Fear of the unknown is part of change. As a new SMT member, you will face uncertainty and ambiguity in results. This is natural and to be expected. From your new level of commitment, you may feel overwhelmed by the technical demands, pressures to organise quickly, and social pressures – the result of rocking the traditional boat. Your team should anticipate stress and plan ways to cope with it.

Change challenges people in power

As you experience the ripples of change, so too, will those around you. As you begin to function with increased independence, you may threaten existing authority and influence power structure. Those in power may perceive a loss of power or feel that they have been separated from influential people. They are then likely to offer resistance to your SMT in subtle but potentially damaging ways. They may delay signing SMT requests or find reasons not to attend your meetings. SMT members have opportunities to interact with levels of management which are higher than they would be dealing with in traditional structures. Handle this opportunity with great care.

Change makes the natives restless

Your SMT does not conform to the norm. When you form SMTs, you are deviating from the normal way of doing things. Traditionally, one of the cornerstones of organisational functioning is the establishment of consistent behaviour among its members. SMTs demand unconventional behaviour from their members so you should expect pressure from colleagues and peers.

Rules and regulations governing the organisation may have to be bent to accommodate what you are doing. Performance evaluations, signing for expenditure etc may require the modification of existing administrative norms. When this happens, expect that many friends and colleagues will uphold the *status quo* and side with traditional ways of operating. In a sense, you find out more about your friends. When you receive support, express your gratitude for it. When your colleagues do not provide support, put it down to encountering the obstacles of change. You and your team members will need to be completely committed to becoming an SMT, because the 'school of tradition' will very likely be on the warpath to prevent your doing so.

After your team has shared the wisdom of the scroll, you should plan a meeting to discuss each potential member's readiness to meet the challenge of change. The change machine has given you much to think about. You need some time together to digest its words. Part 2 provides guidelines to help you evaluate your readiness to form a solid front against the obstacles likely to be promoted by the *status quo*.

Review

1. In this chapter, what is the most important piece of information you received about change?

_____

_____

_____

_____

_____

_____

2. How do you feel about making the changes you will need to make to be involved in an SMT?

_____

_____

_____

_____

_____

_____

_____

3. How would you handle a situation in which a colleague or peer challenged your participation in an SMT?

_____

_____

_____

_____

_____

_____

_____

CHAPTER 7
Rewards and Benefits

Recent studies show that employee satisfaction is higher in SMTs than in traditional employee/manager relationships. Today's employees expect a reasonable income, but they also expect 'psychic income', gained from satisfaction in their work. This psychological wage is gaining increasing importance as well-educated groups have high expectations of personal fulfilment but face an organisational 'flattening' which leaves available fewer top management positions to use their talents.

Nevertheless, employees today seek challenge, responsibility and the feeling of 'making a difference'. Nurses, accountants, local authority employees – all are demanding that their jobs provide them not only with a decent living but also with opportunities for growth and job satisfaction. Employees experience an increased sense of self-worth from doing a good job. Increased self-esteem is an important motivator. It validates us as human beings. It says, 'I am important'. 'I am valued.' 'I am competent.'

Self-esteem at work comes from

Autonomy

Accepting responsibility

Accomplishment

A feeling of belonging

Self-esteem survey

As you consider your participation in an SMT, you may want to check your current 'esteem quotient'. Complete the following survey now, then complete it again after six months of participation in your SMT to see how much your psychic income has increased. We expect that you will notice a considerable difference and will be moving 'full esteem ahead!'

Today's esteem quotient					
Rating scale: 1 = Lowest score (big problem)					
5 = Highest score (no problem)					
1. I am motivated to do my best work each day.	1	2	3	4	5
2. I feel appreciated by my colleagues.	1	2	3	4	5
3. I receive credit for the responsibility I assume.	1	2	3	4	5
4. I have a feeling of accomplishment in my work.	1	2	3	4	5
5. I am free to make decisions and act on them.	1	2	3	4	5
6. I am good at solving problems.	1	2	3	4	5
7. I am comfortable with increased responsibility.	1	2	3	4	5
8. I have confidence in my abilities.	1	2	3	4	5
9. Learning new skills is exciting and challenging.	1	2	3	4	5
10. I am productive most of the time.	1	2	3	4	5
11. I have a strong team spirit.	1	2	3	4	5
12. I work in a climate of caring and trust.	1	2	3	4	5
13. My work provides psychological satisfaction.	1	2	3	4	5
14. I am committed to my work.	1	2	3	4	5
15. I support my organisation's goals.	1	2	3	4	5

Esteem quotient
(To be completed six months after you have formed your SMT)

Rating scale: 1 = Lowest score (big problem)
5 = Highest score (no problem)

1. I am motivated to do my best work each day.   1 2 3 4 5

2. I feel appreciated by my colleagues.   1 2 3 4 5

3. I receive credit for the responsibility I assume.   1 2 3 4 5

4. I have a feeling of accomplishment in my work.   1 2 3 4 5

5. I am free to make decisions and act on them.   1 2 3 4 5

6. I am good at solving problems.   1 2 3 4 5

7. I am comfortable with increased responsibility.   1 2 3 4 5

8. I have confidence in my abilities.   1 2 3 4 5

9. Learning new skills is exciting and challenging.   1 2 3 4 5

10. I am productive most of the time.   1 2 3 4 5

11. I have a strong team spirit.   1 2 3 4 5

12. I work in a climate of caring and trust.   1 2 3 4 5

13. My work provides psychological satisfaction.   1 2 3 4 5

14. I am committed to my work.   1 2 3 4 5

15. I support my organisation's goals.   1 2 3 4 5

Organisational benefits of SMTs

When employee satisfaction increases, organisations reap benefits from SMT success. If they didn't they would have no reason to implement SMTs in the first place. The manager of Production Resources at General Electric Company, USA states that when you combine automation with new systems and SMTs, you reap a 40 to 50 per cent increase in quality and productivity. Increases may vary depending on circumstances and the maturity of the SMT scheme, but these percentages are encouraging manufacturing firms, banks, insurance companies and others to establish SMTs. Listed overleaf are several benefits of SMTs for organisations who have tried them. Tick those that apply to your organisation if you are already involved in SMTs. If you are not, place a cross in those that you would like to have happen as a result of installing SMTs.

☐ Increased employee satisfaction

☐ Greater productivity (30 per cent average)

☐ Job commitment

☐ Commitment to the organisation

☐ Increased individual effort towards stated goals

☐ Motivation through peer pressure rather than mandates from the top

☐ Less need for management intervention (policing attitude)

☐ Increased employee development

☐ Flexible work practices

☐ Employees who are capable of doing more than one job

☐ More appreciation for quality control.

Caution: SMTs may be habit-forming

Once employees have experienced the benefits of SMTs, they may not want to return to traditional structures. When you create SMTs, you create a shift in consciousness that moves people to new levels of growth. When enough SMTs are functioning effectively the entire organisation experiences a sense of urgency that demands positive action.

Note to managers. Once an organisation has adopted SMTs as alternatives to traditional work structures, it will not be able to return to the old ways easily. Most employees are so pleased with their new roles that morale would suffer greatly if the SMTs were dissolved.

Once employees experience autonomy, responsibility,

accomplishment and a feeling of belonging, SMTs can't be discontinued without negative consequences. SMTs *are* habit-forming, so the organisation must be firmly committed from the beginning to the long-term objectives of supporting SMTs from their infancy to their natural conclusions.

Review

1. What is the greatest personal reward in working in an SMT?

_____

_____

_____

_____

_____

_____

2. What is the greatest benefit to your organisation?

_____

_____

_____

_____

_____

_____

_____

_____

_____

PART 2
Getting Started

Part 2 provides some important considerations for you and your team to address as a way of evaluating your readiness for forming an SMT. Please begin this section by working together and writing out your answers to the following questions. Read each question, then answer it according to your current knowledge and opinions about your team and its readiness to become an SMT. Following your answer are the authors' comments. Read them after you have written your opinion. We hope that our comments broaden your perspective and help direct your thinking.

CHAPTER 8
Readiness Assessment

1. Are you willing to succeed or fail as a team?

Authors' comments

SMT members must have an 'All for one and one for all' attitude. Successful SMTs inevitably say that a critical point in their formation was when they made the commitment to do things as a team and live with the results – good *or* bad. Because your individual success depends on the team, members are motivated to do whatever is necessary, such as cover for someone when required. Very often this kind of support is necessary.

Team spirit and cooperation are essential in an SMT. They create a climate for accomplishing tasks and a sense of cohesiveness that allows everyone to feel connected. This cohesiveness acts as a 'social glue' which holds the team together through difficult times.

2. Are you willing to use and accept peer pressure as a means of control within the team?

Authors' comments

As a result of explicit team commitment, members will feel a high degree of peer pressure for task accomplishment. You have no formal leader or conventional command and control power chain to induce you to do your jobs. Your greatest source of control is peer pressure. For peer pressure to work effectively and positively, people must feel connected with the team in more than an administrative sense. They must feel that *their* success is tied to the *team's* success.

3. Is there a climate of trust within the team?

Authors' comments

You will function in a mutually dependent relationship. Your professional credibility and career progress is affected by the product your team produces. You make yourselves professionally vulnerable to each other. Unless you are willing to be equally vulnerable, the SMT process will fail. What are you doing to foster trust?

Trust has two components: (1) You must be able to trust; and (2) You must perceive that your team members are trustworthy. These components interact. When you place your trust in others, you are making yourself vulnerable. If group members are defensive and always covering their tracks, trust breaks down. Additionally, group members must perceive each other as capable, dependable, predictable and as acting with integrity. You must have the group's best interests in mind at all times. Trust can always be strengthened, but in the very beginning a core of trust must exist to ensure the team's success.

4. Have you clearly discussed your expectations, and are they realistic?

Authors' comments

Conflict arises from failed expectations. When you feel that your expectations have not been met, you feel hurt or betrayed. Then you get angry, and anger produces conflict. Expectations are often implicit, that is, they are not made public. We assume that others know what we expect because our expectations are so obvious to us. Remember this rule of thumb. Carve it into your desks, write it a hundred times on your computer screen. *When operating in a team, you can never be too clear!* From the outset, potential SMT members must take the time to *identify*, *discuss* and *agree* their expectations of what their SMT will be and how it will operate.

Don't forget reality. Agreement is not enough. You must also be realistic. Knowing what is reasonable for your unique situation is critical. You will want to examine carefully the reasons for individual members' conclusions, as well. Plan to approach the topic of expectations and reasons with your eyes wide open, your ears tuned in, and your hearts open for honest communication.

5. Do you each have personal and/or professional benefits to gain from joining an SMT

Authors' comments

When you commit yourself to an SMT, you are acknowledging its value and your willingness to do what is necessary to make it succeed. For making this commitment, you will want some kind of pay-off. You should give serious consideration to the age-old question, 'What's in it for me (us)?'

You are changing many things in your personal operating style, including delaying gratification of personal needs and operating with a higher degree of uncertainty. To make these sacrifices, you must believe the rewards are worth the effort involved. If each team member cannot establish clear benefits for himself or herself, regardless of how other members feel, they will not be able to sustain their initial effort. Readiness is low. List below as many personal and team benefits and advantages as you can think of. Review pages 53–57 to see if you can add others to complete your list.

6. **Are you willing to pay attention to *how* you do things as well as *what* you do?**

> **Authors' comments**
> As a leaderless group, you will need to pay close attention to your process. *How* you do things matters as much as *what* you do, especially in the beginning. By developing a good task process, you contribute greatly to the group's effectiveness, and therefore its productivity. When you begin to feel productive, output increases, and so does group cohesiveness. You feel good about your product and about each other.
>
> In addition to a well-defined task process, you must establish and abide by interpersonal ground rules (group norms and standards of behaviour). Describe behaviour codes explicitly and in writing and then submit them to the group for its approval. These norms will prevent breaches of conduct down the line. You will need to evaluate yourselves periodically to check members' compliance with the codes. Your SMT's success depends upon the integrity of the relationships among its members. Take relationships seriously; then monitor your process as well as your outcomes.

7. **Are you willing to engage in long-term thinking?**

> **Authors' comments**
> One SMT member stated in an interview, 'I'm not sure why I should spend so much time and effort with an SMT if I'm really not going to be part of the team for the duration.' Her comment reflects the fluid state of most organisations. People move frequently, and if they believe they may be part of a team for a relatively short time, they may not be willing to invest much time and effort into it. It is a fact that if people leave a group the SMT can continue to function. However, if people join an SMT with the idea, 'If it doesn't go well, I won't be here long anyway', or 'I'll be able to leave it easily enough', the group spirit will be deeply affected. You need to make decisions and exert effort with the expectation that you will be living with the outcome for a long time.

The final three questions on your readiness review are practical rather than philosophical. They are, however, just as important in evaluating your readiness for an SMT as the previous questions. In fact, you cannot begin your group until you have answered them.

8. To what extent do you function without management now?

Authors' comments

If a team has had no experience working together as a group, you may not be able to judge your potential for doing so. Groups who have operated somewhat autonomously or who have worked with a highly participatory manager are stronger candidates for becoming fully functioning SMTs.

9. Do you have a sponsor?

Authors' comments

As already explained, you must have the support of senior management in order to succeed. Management demonstrates its readiness for SMTs by willingly designating someone in authority to sponsor an SMT. That person can help you to hurdle administrative and political blocks.

10. **Do you possess the required technical, administrative and interpersonal skills you need?**

Authors' comments

In order to be successful, an SMT needs its members to possess all the requisite skills. This includes administrative skills as well as specific technical expertise. Letters and reports must be written; the budget must be monitored; schedules must be devised, and tracking procedures formulated. Team members will be sharing many of these responsibilities, particularly the ones usually handled by managers. If you have no interest in administration or lack administrative skills, you may have to force yourself to become interested in these matters and learn how to carry your share of the administrative load. If you do not assume your fair share of tasks and responsibilities, it is likely to create dissension within the team.

You will also need to fine-tune your interpersonal skills. You must be able to listen, participate effectively, argue a position without taking things personally or becoming defensive, resolve conflict, solve problems, etc. These are all critical skills that will help your SMT to survive its start-up phase of defining relationships and expectations.

Review

1. What is the most important piece of information you discovered in your readiness review?

_____

_____

_____

_____

_____

_____

_____

2. What are you going to do with this information?

_____

_____

_____

_____

_____

_____

_____

_____

3. What areas do you need to discuss further to gain more information or solve existing problems?

_____

_____

_____

_____

_____

_____

_____

_____

CHAPTER 9

A Smart Start for
Self-managing teams

Once you and your work group have decided to become an SMT, you will want to know how to 'start smart'. Actually, you have taken the first step by agreeing to work together. Your teamwork and cooperation are the most critical elements for your success. Now, you must make some practical decisions to help you move ahead. Listed below are suggestions for a smart start. In the space at the end of this section jot down those items on your personal 'To do' list for getting started.

Plan your SMT

You and your group are faced with the challenge of combining highly fragmented jobs usually performed by individuals into natural work units, with teams responsible for a product or service. You are redesigning the traditional system to maximise your involvement, growth and efficiency. Tick those activities you have completed.

☐ Spoken to key managers and employees who will be involved in planning

☐ Identified your customers and established a means of direct contact with them

☐ Discussed your customers' needs with them

☐ Set weekly goals for discussing and meeting customers' needs and for obtaining feedback from them

- ☐ Identified your competitors
- ☐ Set standards for quality, quantity, cost and schedules
- ☐ Designed clear measurements for output
- ☐ Designed job descriptions to execute operational tasks
- ☐ Developed charts and diagrams to plot your progress
- ☐ Designed jobs to execute management and co-ordination tasks, ie scheduling, task assignments, recruitment, cross-training
- ☐ Outlined the responsibilities of each job
- ☐ Identified the additional information you need and decided how you will get it.

Spend adequate time planning. Visualise what your team will look like in five years' time. Be sure your planning activities are based on your written goals.

Now you try it!

To do:

_____

_____

_____

_____

_____

Write a proposal

You need management approval to organise an SMT. You will have the best chance of securing it if you present management with a well-written proposal. Clear writing reflects clear thinking. The proposal is a selling tool and, as such, it should provide a precise statement of your SMT's benefit to the organisation. Your proposal should include:

- A 'what' and 'why' statement (What is an SMT and why is it important?)
- Why an SMT is needed and how that need originated
- Why meeting the need is important
- What results you hope to achieve
- How you will achieve them
- In what form you plan to present your results
- What you will need from management (costs, support, materials)
- What the benefits to the company are in adopting SMTs
- What the SMT will cost the organisation

Write your proposal with your reader(s) in mind. What do they need to know? In what manner are they accustomed to receiving proposals? What will you need to prove, to those with the authority to make the final decisions? Your proposal will help you and your team to clarify your purpose and define your scope. Once you have secured upper management's approval, you will be able to form your SMT.

To do:

_____

_____

_____

_____

_____

Write contracts

If together you can write a sound contract, you have a good chance of succeeding as an SMT. You should write separate team contracts, individual contracts, and a contract with your sponsor.

Your contracts should include the rules under which your team (and you) will function. *You will return to your contract many times for clarification and direction.* It will be your primary tool for solving day-to-day problems and disputes. The contract should be a 'living document' that you can change or upgrade as you grow. Your SMT is a process of personal and group development and should evolve into greater areas of responsibility as the group matures. Your contracts should reflect your evolution. They should include:

- Your SMT creed. What do you believe about SMTs? What does the contract mean to you and to your fellow team members?
- What the SMTs agree to do. (Be very specific: 'A member of the ABC team will attend the DEF planning meeting each week.' 'We will submit a weekly project schedule report to the group project leader.')
- Your goal as an SMT. 'We plan to complete Phase I of the Alpha Project by 1 June 199X.'
- Results of failure to comply to the terms of the contract.

Chapter 12 provides additional help in writing your contract.

To do:

_____

_____

_____

_____

_____

_____

Specify your upper level manager contact

You will need a compatible upper level manager to help you obtain information and to support your team's decisions. You should report regularly to him or her for feedback. You may be assigned a head of division or perhaps a director. Write a contract with this person to clarify your mutual roles. You can also designate an additional 'development manager' to help the team plan and develop, although he or she is not responsible for production. In the beginning, the development manager acts as an adviser or coach but has no management authority. The team may outgrow the need for a development manager as it matures.

To do:

_____

_____

_____

_____

_____

_____

Keep your SMT small

Small groups (five to nine members) can communicate more effectively than large ones. If a large department wishes to develop SMTs, it can establish several small units divided according to task. Each group can designate a leader who is responsible for communicating with the other group leaders.

To do:

_____

_____

_____

_____

_____

_____

Fine-tune your communication skills

Take time to evaluate how well you communicate. Tick the skills listed below that you already possess.

- ☐ Are you a good listener?
- ☐ Can people trust what you say?
- ☐ Do you provide feedback to ensure mutual understanding?
- ☐ Do you provide verbal and non-verbal evidence that you have heard and understood what someone has said?
- ☐ Do you avoid jumping to conclusions?
- ☐ Do you ask for additional information when you aren't sure if you know all the facts?
- ☐ Do you speak clearly and distinctly?
- ☐ Can you write clearly?
- ☐ Are you patient?

Most organisations offer classes to help people improve their communication skills. The people who are most successful in SMTs are successful communicators.

To do:

_____

_____

Examine your values

Most organisations take on people who reflect the ideas and values of upper management. Does your organisation have core values of fairness, openness, trust and participation? Do you? Do you have a strong desire to cooperate with other people and achieve mutual goals, or would you rather work alone? If you prefer to work alone, you will not be comfortable in an SMT. SMTs depend on peer pressure. Group values predominate, and you will be observed closely. Your team mates want to know that you are doing your share; you will hear from them if you aren't! The old expression, 'If you can't stand the heat, get out of the kitchen,' holds true in SMTs.

To do:

_____

_____

_____

_____

Establish 'How are we doing?' sessions

Planning regular review sessions to check your progress will help you to stay on track. You will want to review your contracts, assess your timetable to be sure you are on schedule with your work, listen to each team member's progress report, and discuss challenges and disappointments. Be sure to reward yourselves for work well done. Consider a restaurant meal, special T-shirts, recognition posters with your pictures on them. These meetings are a means of auditing your progress. You should schedule them regularly, and they should be held in addition to regular staff meetings.

To do:

_____

_____

_____

_____

_____

Review

1. What suggestions in this section are most important for your team at this time?

   _____

   _____

   _____

   _____

   _____

2. Rank order your *To do* list, placing your most important priorities first, next most important second, etc.

   _____

   _____

   _____

   _____

   _____

3. How would you evaluate your progress towards becoming a fully functioning SMT at this point? Put an X on the line to show your progress.

   Non-existent   Fully functioning

   ├──┤

CHAPTER 10
Ensuring Your Success

The secret of your success lies in your planning. Take the time necessary to plan in four key areas:

1. The internal management and co-ordination of your team
2. Boundary management – how you interact with the rest of the organisation
3. How you will access information
4. What support system you will require.

Each key area deserves special consideration to ensure that you are prepared to meet your needs – including that of survival! Following is a discussion of each key area and your team's responsibilities in each.

Internal management and co-ordination

In addition to your technical jobs, your team will perform many management functions, and you will control the way they are accomplished. You will have more or less freedom, depending on your readiness and your contract agreements with upper management.

Your team must define specific roles that must be filled to manage the day-to-day affairs of the group. These roles, which are administratively based, are designed to meet the operating needs of the group, as well as the demands of the organisation.

Listed on the next page are possible management functions your team might perform. Tick those your team will manage and note to what extent they will do so: Full Responsibility (final decision); Partial Responsibility (make recommendations); or No

Responsibility (performed by upper management). Also note who will assume these responsibilities and for what period.

Internal management checklist			
Task	Extent	Who is responsible	Length of time
Scheduling and co-ordination of group and individual tasks			
Setting goals and objectives			
Writing work plans			
Planning your budget			
Securing your budget			
Forecasting and planning			
Reviewing performance data			
Writing performance data			
Salary administration			
Voucher and expense approvals			
Developing training plans			
Screening applicants			
Interviewing job candidates			
Recruiting new SMT members			
Inducting new members			
Evaluating new team members during probationary periods			
Coaching, developing, providing career guidance			
Cross-training and new skill acquisition			
Terminating team members			
Representing your SMT at important meetings			
Others			

You can make extra copies of the checklist to use as assignment sheets as you trade roles among yourselves. You will want to share these responsibilities in order to learn new skills and prevent boredom. Also, some tasks will be easier than others.

Boundary management

Boundary management comes into play in your interactions with others outside your SMT. When a group functions under traditional management, individuals in other departments know who to contact with questions. Additionally, written communication is often directed to the manager for dissemination, action or a decision. In an SMT this absence of an 'official' manager can cause confusion. One key role in boundary management is the 'Single Point of Contact' (SPOC).

The role of SPOC
The Single Point of Contact (SPOC) funnels phone calls, enquiries, requests and post to the people best able to deal with them. There should be a physical location where the SPOC can be reached by phone or post. The name of the person playing the SPOC role (and his or her location) must be communicated to individuals and groups both within and outside the organisation who have reason to contact your SMT.

The SPOC role can be rotated among team members. One person does not have to commit him- or herself to it indefinitely. If you do rotate, however, be careful to communicate the change to the rest of the organisation. Do not rotate too often, or you will cause confusion and frustration.

Boundary management will need to be negotiated in two areas in which you will be dependent on others outside your SMT: the technical and political spheres. You will need technical assistance on task-related issues that affect other SMTs, groups, projects, individuals or departments. You may find a 'dependencies' chart useful to depict all your interactions where boundary management is an issue. A visual display of your business interfaces is a good way to show these relationships. This display will help you to think through who needs to be part of your information flow.

The next page contains an example of a dependencies chart.

As part of boundary management, you will also need to take into account the political realities of your organisation. Which relationships will you nourish and how will you go about it? And which relationships will nourish you?

Power is the underlying force in organisational politics. Power, or the ability to influence outcomes, can be formal or informal. Formal power, or power *given* to individuals and organisations, is power in its most visible form.

Informal power can be wielded even when people have not been endowed by other authority. To realise your goals, you will need the support of other people. Establishing supportive allies who possess the power to help you is important to your SMT's existence and growth.

How to support your political alliances

Share your SMT vision and goals.
Let your supporters know you appreciate them.
Tell your supporters what they are doing for you.
Tell your supporters who your adversaries are, and why.
Tell your supporters about the problems you are facing.
Ask your supporters for their input and continuing support.
Help your supporters as often as possible, even when they don't ask for help.
Stay in touch.

Identifying task dependencies

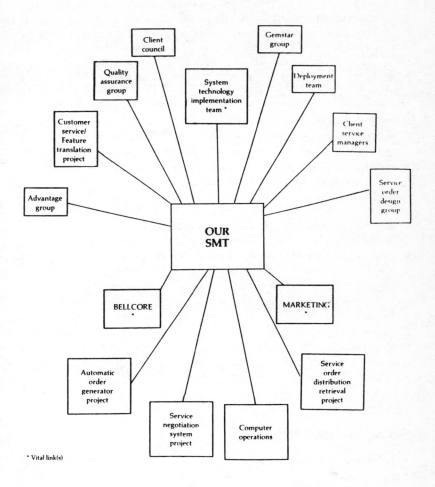

* Vital link(s)

Brian plays politics

Brian is a legal researcher in a large law firm. He is a member of an SMT that interacts regularly with important, highly specialised contractors. At times, the contractors' demands on Brian's SMT are very difficult to meet. The team is currently under pressure from the contractors to complete research on an important case in time for a forthcoming trial.

Brian's team has asked him to negotiate with the contractors for additional resources to meet the deadline. Brian is the obvious person for this job, because he has worked closely with the contractors and developed a strong rapport with them. He has also taken care to include the contractors in many business and social functions.

Brian also interacts well with his team's sponsor. He informs the sponsor regularly about the team's successes, asks the sponsor for advice, and looks for opportunities to show appreciation for the sponsor's support. Because Brian cultivates his team's political alliances, he is able to persuade the SMT sponsor to negotiate with the contractors for additional resources. Brian used his influence (informal power) to persuade two entities (formal powers) to negotiate an outcome favourable for the SMT. When the resources are obtained, Brian will invite the contractors, his team and their sponsor to a Friday afternoon get together to express the team's appreciation of the additional resources.

Access to information

Feedback and evaluation are crucial for self-management. Your SMT needs to consider how it will gain access to needed information. Identify what information you will need, when you will need it, where to find it, and how to obtain it.

In traditional structures, a designated manager facilitates the flow of information. 'Who is doing what?', 'What information is the chairman of the organisation passing down?' 'What is the latest news on our customers?' These kinds of day-to-day question must also be answered by SMTs but without the help of a manager or supervisor. You need to work together and inform each other as you uncover important information about the organisation. SMTs will often expand the SPOC role so that the individuals assuming it also represent them in external information sessions. Other SMT groups, however, choose to be represented by a contract manager.

Contracted manager: a special role
In some situations, a contract (stand-in manager) may be necessary on a temporary basis. A contracted manager functions at the management level to which the SMT would traditionally report. This person understands the SMT process and is sympathetic to it. When requested by the SMT, a contracted manager agrees to serve as the formal manager. Contract managers may be asked:

- To represent SMTs in meetings requiring formal managerial representation
- To pass on administrative information to which only the next higher level would have access
- To negotiate on behalf of the group with senior managers
- To clear political hurdles by speaking to other managers seeking to discuss SMT concerns or problems with someone at their own level
- To arbitrate or 'cast the deciding vote' in close group decisions
- To provide discipline when established counselling and discipline ground rules have failed to eliminate a problem among team members
- To counsel and advise on group tasks and management issues.

The role of the contracted manager must be negotiated among SMT members, the potential contract manager, and the upper level of management sponsoring the SMT. The sponsor could assume the contract manager's role; however, the sponsor is usually a more senior person.

Joe's dilemma
Joe was assigned to attend a high-level managers' meeting as the

SPOC from his SMT. At the meeting, stares and negative glances indicated that he was considered out of place at the meeting. Feeling intimidated, he neither asked questions nor listened carefully to the discussion. After the meeting, several managers instructed him to remain quiet about what he had heard, for they were not ready to announce their plans to the entire organisation. Consequently, Joe was not able to take back any information to his SMT. What could Joe have done differently in order to benefit from the meeting?

Authors' comments

Joe should have asked his SMT sponsor or contracted manager to serve as the 'ears' of his SMT. Upper-level managers would feel comfortable in the meeting, and they would be able to provide appropriate feedback to the team on issues that concerned them. If the sponsor could not attend, Joe should have contacted the person who called the meeting, indicating that he would be attending and his purpose in doing so.

Support systems

Support systems issues are not directly task issues, but they are ultimately important to the SMT. Support system issues include:

- *Career progression.* How will individuals learn and employ the various skills required by the team? What will be the criteria for promotions? How are recommendations for career progression made?
- *Training and development.* How will team members be trained? Who should receive training? What kind of training should be offered? How will training decisions be made? What training does the team need as a whole? What training should be mandatory? What training should be elective?
- *Compensation and rewards.* Who will decide on pay increases? What kind of rewards are available? Should they be based on individual performance or team performance?

You will need to establish ground rules to define your support system. Some issues may be resolved as part of internal management issues. Others will not fit into that category and should be addressed separately. Use your own resources and those of others to resolve these issues.

Where to look for help
- *Other teams.* Some SMTs may already have considered your support systems issues and could advise you on them.
- *Human resource professionals.* These specialists can help in such areas as team member training and development.
- *Administrative rules.* Some issues, such as remuneration packages, may be treated in previous administrative decisions. Certain issues are likely to be tightly controlled, leaving you little flexibility for creating your own process. Identify constraints and plan to live with them cheerfully while you develop your plan. You will always have to live within certain organisational limits and management desires.

Action items

Review with your team these four key areas: internal management, boundary management, accessing information and support systems. On the checklist below, indicate those items you are doing now and those you plan to do. In the space below indicate other readiness actions you have taken and those you plan to take.

Already doing	Will do	
☐	☐	Identify all internal management roles your team will require.
☐	☐	Designate the extent of team responsibility in each role.
☐	☐	Contract with upper management to assign management roles and their administration to your SMT.

Already doing	Will do	
☐	☐	Assign a SPOC for the team.
☐	☐	Define the role of SPOC and the length of time an individual will assume the role.
☐	☐	Communicate to others in the organisation who is serving as SPOC and how to contact him or her.
☐	☐	Create a dependencies chart, identifying all boundary interactions. (This may change often.)
☐	☐	Identify all important political alliances.
☐	☐	Develop a strategy for cultivating political alliances.
☐	☐	Identify all organisational information you need to function effectively.
☐	☐	Meet SPOC and/or your sponsor to discuss information needs.
☐	☐	List specific means of satisfying your information needs.
☐	☐	Identify all outside support systems. (These may change often.)
☐	☐	Define what support you can expect from each group.

Here's what else you are doing:

_____

_____

_____

Here's what else you intend to do:

_____

_____

_____

Review

1. In which readiness areas is your team strongest?

_____

_____

_____

_____

_____

_____

2. In which areas do you need more focus?

_____

_____

_____

_____

_____

3. What is your next readiness step?

_____

_____

_____

_____

_____

4. How will you accomplish it?

_____

_____

_____

_____

_____

_____

_____

_____

_____

PART 3
Rounding Out Your Resources

CHAPTER 11
Self-managing Teams' Facilitative Skills

As you go into business as an SMT, you can anticipate many of the problems that might occur and even plan their solutions. How you seek those solutions – the manner in which you solve problems, gain agreement, correct errors and follow your process – are your facilitative skills. These skills can be taught, learned, changed and reviewed as needed. They are basic tools needed by your SMT day in and day out. Without them, you would feel as if you were running a race wearing only one shoe.

This chapter addresses four facilitative skills you need to master to enable your SMT to sit, stand, walk and run. From your first steps until you break the tape crossing the finish line, you will use these skills over and over.

- Problem-solving
- Gaining consensus
- Self-correction
- Managing process.

Check your perception

Before reading what follows, check your current perceptions of these four facilitative skills. Place a 'T' next to those statements you think are true and an 'F' next to those you think are false. When you have read the information in this chapter, go back and check your answers again. Have you changed your mind about any of your answers? If you are still not sure, see the answers on page 93.

True or False

1. _____ Open-ended problems (several interrelated, intangible issues) are more difficult to solve than close-ended problems (single answer issues).

2. _____ Individuals are generally better than groups at solving open-ended problems.

3. _____ When gaining consensus, the discussion is less important than the outcome.

4. _____ Conflict and tension are unnecessary in problem-solving and decision-making.

5. _____ Consensus means 100 per cent agreement.

6. _____ Defensiveness and finger-pointing are part of the self-correcting process.

7. _____ Ground rules are acceptable but not essential for an SMT.

8. _____ You can never be too obvious or explicit when clarifying your purpose and outcome.

9. _____ When monitoring team members' performance in your SMT, content and personalities go hand in hand.

10. _____ Political power, expert power and personal power are all factors of influence in SMTs.

Answers

1. T. 2. F (Groups are better at solving open-ended problems, because they bring to the solution more information and experience.) 3. F (Consensus is a process, not an outcome, so both are equally important. All ideas must be heard and understood.) 4. F (Conflicting ideas are essential to problem-solving and decision-making. These interchanges can naturally result in tension and conflict, and groups must learn to manage them.) 5. F (Consensus occurs when everyone has been heard, agreement has been obtained, and everyone has committed him- or herself to his or her role in implementing the decision.) 6. T. 7. F (Ground rules establishing norms and standards allow groups to perform their tasks effectively and enable their members to grow and develop. Without ground rules, teams cannot function.) 8. T. 9. F (You must learn to separate problems from personalities if you are to be successful in the self-correcting process.) 10. T.

Self-managing means problem-solving

As a member of an SMT you will be solving both technical and non-technical problems. As a result, you will be solving two types of problem, close-ended and open-ended.

Close-ended problems

We were taught to solve close-ended problems at school. Close-ended problems have single correct solutions or sets of solutions. Often you don't even need to test the solution. If asked to add two plus two, everyone on your team knows the answer is four. If your SMT only had to solve close-ended problems, your jobs would be very simple. The following questions will help you to decide if a problem is close-ended:

- How much do we know about the problem?
- Do we have complete and adequate information? Is it quantifiable?
- Do technical or procedural methods already exist for solving the problem?

The more questions you have answered affirmatively, the more likely you are to be faced with a close-ended problem. These problems are not usually difficult for teams to solve. In fact, individual experts within the group can usually handle close-ended problems themselves, without calling upon the decision-making/problem-solving capabilities of the team as a whole. Open-ended problems are another matter!

Open-ended problems

Open-ended problems do not offer rose-strewn paths to their solutions. Information about the problem is ambiguous or missing altogether. Often, open-ended problems are really a nest of problems. Like a jigsaw puzzle, they are inter-connecting pieces which must be taken apart and viewed separately. How do you change the culture of an organisation? Each part of the culture is a piece of the puzzle. Taking it apart and changing it creates a new picture. There is no one 'correct' answer. The only 'correct' answer to an open-ended problem is the answer that works best.

When you work with open-ended problems, you will usually find more than one workable solution. Sometimes, two good solutions will be antithetical. Open-ended problems can be messy. Because they have more than one moving part, they often confound the system. You can't guarantee solutions in advance. The process of solving them is one of trial and error. Educated trial and error works best. Most SMT problems will be open ended. Open-ended problems are best solved by teams.

The superiority of problem-solving teams

Groups are best suited for making decisions and solving problems that have no single correct, or best, answer. Teams bring more information and experience to the problem. In this case, two, three, four or more heads are better than one.

Because open-ended problems have no *external* means for validating solutions, the sole criterion for correctness is the team's acceptance of the decision as correct. Team members process and filter information to test, refine and finally select the best solution. Consensus is the best approach for solving open-ended problems.

Questions for discussion
1. What are some of the open-ended problems facing your SMT now?
2. What steps are you taking to solve these problems?
3. How can you use your team members' expertise to solve these problems?
4. Have you planned a method for gaining consensus?

Remember
The only correct answer to an open-ended problem is the answer that works best.

Self-managing means gaining consensus

'Can we get a consensus on that?', 'What is the consensus here?', 'The consensus was that we start the next phase.' The word 'consensus' is often used in organisations. Often it is misused and misunderstood. Like the word 'communication', 'consensus' is used by everyone, but it means different things to different people. For your SMT, you will want to have a common understanding of the *practical application* of consensus. Some guidelines follow. Following each guideline, finish the statement with respect to your SMT. If your SMT is already formed and functioning, describe how you are following, or plan to follow, this guideline. If you are in the planning stages of your SMT, describe how you will use each guideline to help you to get started. If you have specific results from following each guideline, write a statement describing those results.

Consensus is a process, not an outcome. In an SMT, consensus includes discussing openly and honestly team members' ideas and concerns. The discussion, not just the outcome, is important. Since your SMT has no official 'decision maker', each person has a right to speak openly in an attempt to influence the outcomes.

In a consensual process, ideas must be heard – and *understood*. Be sure to probe the reasons behind each team member's statement, so that everyone understands the thinking process as well as the proposed conclusions.

In your SMT, the consensual process . . .

Results:

_____

_____

_____

_____

_____

_____

_____

Everyone is equal – but some are more equal than others. While everyone has an opportunity to influence the group, some will be more influential than others. Your influence will depend on the particular issue, idea, problem or decision you are discussing, *and* the type of power that the group perceives you to have at that particular time. Your influence derives from different power bases. Following are descriptions of three important power bases that influence SMTs:

1. *Expertise* is one source of influence. You are accorded power when the group believes that you have knowledge or expertise about a subject, usually in well-defined areas. You may be an expert in solving administrative problems, but if the subject shifts to technical areas, the power base will shift to other members with technical expertise.
2. A second power source is *personal credibility*. When team members perceive that you are motivated to act in the best

interests of the team, your personal credibility increases. If certain members are well-liked or team members identify with them in some way, their credibility is enhanced. Additionally, if you possess good interpersonal skills (listening to others, asking relevant questions, supporting others' ideas), you may have more influence on the group.

3. *Political power* is a third source of influence. Team members possess political power when fellow team members perceive another member as having informal influence within the organisation that can make him or her a source of potential rewards or punishments. Cynthia joined an SMT shortly after she left a position as administrative assistant to the Executive Director of Operations in her organisation. Because she had worked for the Director for many years, her team perceived that she had political contacts that could help or hurt their SMT. Such a source of power can give people's words more weight. Political influence can hurt a team only if the team's process becomes too politically motivated.

In your SMT, you recognise or will recognise the following kinds of influence:

Results:

_____

_____

_____

_____

Consensus does not imply a lack of conflict. A critical exchange of ideas is essential to gaining consensus within the team. When ideas are controversial, conflict and tension may result. *Conflict and tension are natural* in problem-solving and decision-making, so SMT members should expect a healthy amount of it. Think of consensus as controlled conflict that leads to productive solutions.

In your SMT, conflict and tension . . .

Results:

_____

_____

_____

_____

Consensus is not necessarily 100 per cent agreement. In fact, 100 per cent agreement is a myth. Three conditions must exist for consensus to occur:

1. Each member must feel he or she has been heard and understood by the rest of the team.
2. Each member must be able to 'live with' the decision or solution.
3. Each member must be willing to *commit* him- or herself to his or her role in carrying out the decision or implementing the solution.

In our SMT, you determine/will determine consensus by:

Results:

_____

_____

_____

_____

Self-managing means self-correcting

The majority of problems that need solving are open ended, which makes 'perfect' decisions impossible. The process of taking your 'best shot' (your group's consensus), then listening to feedback to self-correct is natural – although frustrating – when solving open-ended problems. You will also want to know what conditions are necessary to be a self-correcting work team.

Self-correcting teams *do* make mistakes, but they correct them. They learn from mistakes, and they don't keep making the same mistakes. By learning as they go, a self-correcting team can generally keep from making a mistake from which they cannot recover. A self-correcting team realises that work, like life, is a continuing education. They allow the educational process to enhance their effectiveness.

To become good at self-correcting is to be willing to confront problems constructively when decisions go awry or solutions fail. The following points will help:

Practise levelling

'Levelling' is the open, frank discussion of problems. Team members must be willing to *speak up* about problems and *listen* to others' perceptions of the problem.

You level most effectively if you are trusted and if you trust fellow team members. People are vulnerable when speaking out about what they perceive. They can only do so in an atmosphere of good faith. Levelling, supported by trust, permits real learning.

Find problems: don't point fingers

When SMT members ask '*Who* is the problem?' rather than '*What* is the problem?' defensiveness and mistrust take over. To be self-correcting, problems must be viewed apart from personalities. Examine the problem objectively and allow your team to learn from it. If people associated with a problem feel they are being attacked, they are tempted to cover up or defend their positions instead of helping to solve the problem. Rational problem-solving requires rational people.

Look carefully at what you are doing

By engaging in process evaluation, you examine not only *what* the team does, but *how* it functions. You are taking time to review the past to plan for the future. All individuals, teams and organisations that wish to grow must take time regularly to determine what is working and what isn't. Evaluate your process; then process your evaluation.

Jennifer learns self-correction

Jennifer is a new member of a well-organised and successful SMT. She has agreed to enrol team members in training courses, in addition to performing her regular job. When Jennifer had difficulty locating the required classes for team members, she decided to enrol them in similar classes that sounded as if they would meet the training requirements. However, she forgot to inform her team about what she had done.

After attending the classes Jennifer had arranged for them, several members complained that they had not received the training they needed and expected. Jennifer realised that she was responsible for people losing time away from their jobs only to return empty-handed.

Because the team atmosphere was supportive, Jennifer risked bringing up the problem and admitting her mistake at the next team meeting. Her team mates listened carefully, then patiently explained the importance of the right training classes to help them gain the expertise required to complete their project on time. The team then took the time to review with Jennifer their training requirements and the classes listed in their training catalogue. In the process, they found two additional classes they could attend to speed up their educational process.

Jennifer levelled with her team, and they responded by examining the problem rather than simply blaming her. Together, they re-evaluated their education process and discovered viable alternatives.

Managing your team's process

When your team gets together to talk, it must examine two components of the discussion: (1) The substance of the discussion; and (2) The process of the discussion. The substance of a discussion is the actual content, or agenda. While content is important, you must also notice *how* you are discussing issues. In other words, what is your process?

Every group has two kinds of process issues to manage: task-process issues and people-process issues. Task-process involves the relationship between team members and their work. People-process involves the relationships of group members to each other. Both issues must be well-managed. Ninety-nine per cent of the problems in SMTs can be traced to poor processing, because the group's output depends on its productivity and cohesiveness. Both are affected by group process.

The importance of ground rules

To be a productive and cohesive team, you must establish ground rules together, and then all agree to abide by them. By paying attention to your ground rules during problem-solving and decision-making sessions, you can increase your effectiveness and save a great deal of time. Use the following suggested ground rules as guidelines to help you establish your own ground rules for your team. The ground rules are not as important in themselves as the ideas they represent with respect to your functioning effectively as a team.

Task-process ground rules

Clarify your purpose and specify your outcomes
Never assume that team members understand the purpose of problem-solving or decision-making sessions. You can never be too obvious or explicit about your desired outcome. Purpose and outcome are two sides of the same coin. Clarifying one clarifies the other.

Seek alternative methods and procedures for achieving your outcomes
Don't get in a rut. Be creative in the way you perform your group tasks. The methods you use to solve one type of problem may not be suitable for another type.

Make your task structure explicit
The task structure is your plan for solving a problem or arriving at a decision. It includes the step-by-step process you will follow for accomplishing your task. First, you should gain consensus

about the steps you will follow, then explicitly formulate them and write them down. This will help you to stay on track. Because you are working with a 'living document', you should feel free to change the structure and add or delete steps when necessary.

Stick to the subject
Just as you must stay on track with the steps in the task structure (unless you want to change them), so must you maintain your focus on the subject. When people work on projects together, their attention spans are notoriously low. Conversations drift like leaves on a pond. Because they are in the same pond, people think they are addressing the same subject. Often, they are not. You can institute a 'subject challenge' to help keep you on track. Whenever you begin to drift, anyone in the group can say 'subject challenge', and you must justify what you are saying and how it relates to your agenda items, and specifically to the subject you are discussing. After having received a few subject challenges, most people stay on track. Be sure to do this with humour and good will to prevent it from becoming punitive.

Summarise
In team discussion, the many conversational threads floating about can weave a tangled web that must be unravelled. Summarising from time to time helps to keep your agenda orderly and lets you know where you stand. Earlier, we stated that you cannot be too explicit when working in a group. Summaries should be especially clear in their expression. Check to see that the group validates the summary as an accurate expression of the process.

Monitor your time
You can easily lose track of time in problem-solving and decision-making discussions, especially if topics are controversial. As you plan your task structure, be sure to include a time structure. You don't have to structure time to the second, a 'guesstimate' will do. But you should have a point of reference for where you should be and the time it is taking to get there.

Identify task assignments and/or 'next steps' at the end of your session
Do not leave your working sessions open ended. As you end the session, summarise who is to do what by when. *Make sure you get verbal commitments from everyone on the actions for which they are responsible.* Also, specify any 'next steps' for the team as a whole. Even if you haven't reached closure on certain issues, you can identify what you need to do to arrive at it. Don't leave things up in the air.

Task ground rules exercise

Review your task ground rules with your team and discuss how well you process each one. Complete the exercise below to identify where you are functioning well and where you need improvement.

	You're doing well			Needs work	
You clarify your purpose and specify outcomes.	1	2	3	4	5
You look for alternatives for achieving outcomes.	1	2	3	4	5
You maintain an explicit task structure.	1	2	3	4	5
You stick to the subject.	1	2	3	4	5
You summarise and check for agreement.	1	2	3	4	5
You monitor your time.	1	2	3	4	5
You identify task assignments and 'next steps'.	1	2	3	4	5

When you have identified your status with your task ground rules, discuss those areas you want to improve and how you can improve them.

You can improve your task ground rules by:

_____

_____   _____

_____

_____

_____

_____

People-process ground rules

People-process ground rules involve your team's relationships with each other. You cannot make hard and fast rules for how you treat each other, but you can establish expectations and adopt ground rules for acceptable behaviour. Tick those items in the following guidelines with which you agree.

☐ *Provide opportunities for everyone to contribute.* People refrain from speaking up in discussions for various reasons: they are shy, other people dominate, they lack expertise, etc. Regardless of this, communication in your team discussions must be reasonably well balanced. Everyone needn't contribute equally, but if people are too quiet for too long, their input should be solicited. Try to maintain a balance, so members won't feel excluded.

☐ *Separate content from personalities.* 'Love me, love my ideas, and if you don't love my ideas, then you don't love me.' *Wrong.* When discussing a team issue, keep the discussion away from personal issues and overtones. Similarly, team members should not take personal offence if someone doesn't approve of their ideas. Mature team members can maintain self-esteem even when others disagree with them. When members take things personally, tempers flare and tasks are forgotten. Each team member and the group as a whole share the important responsibility of remaining professional in discussing controversial topics.

☐ *Protect individuals from personal attack.* In the heat of discussion, comments can be made that damage the self-esteem of group members, who may feel that they are being attacked personally. Nothing destroys team cohesiveness faster than damage to the self-esteem of its members. Even seemingly personal attacks are usually unintentional. If you feel someone is being attacked, stand by and provide them with support. When team members feel that others will stand up for them, the level of trust and the opportunity for open communication are increased.

☐ *Reduce and reconcile misunderstandings and disagreement.* Paradoxically, one problem in communication is that we speak the same language. Because we use the same words, we think we understand each other. This is seldom true. As a team member, listen to group discussion with this key question in mind: 'What are they saying, and what do they mean?' Team members may use the same words to say something different, or use different words to say the same thing. Communication is a tricky business. When legitimate disagreements occur, look for common ground. Remember, if handled constructively, disagreement is a natural and healthy part of the consensual process.

☐ *Provide recognition for the group process.* When your team is solving problems or making decisions, progress is slow. Groups do not work quickly, especially when working by consensus. To avoid frustration, look for opportunities to identify progress. You help to create a positive climate and a sense of achievement that might otherwise be missed.

☐ *Provide a fair hearing for all ideas and comments.* Part of the consensual process is that ideas are shared, listened to, and taken into account by the group. If team members feel that their ideas are ignored or squashed they will feel resentful and defensive and may either withdraw from the discussion or become aggressive in order to be heard. Avoid this by providing a *fair* hearing for all group members. Keep in mind, however, that over-repetition of ideas or beating an issue into the ground is counter-productive. The group should maintain a balance between a willingness to listen and acting decisively.

☐ *Help the group to focus on 'win-win' solutions.* Win/win (or 'all win') solutions occur when team members feel that the decision process has integrity and that their needs were met. To achieve win/win solutions, the group must work hard to build on each other's ideas. 'Either/or' thinking produces winners and losers. Your SMT will be in trouble if team members feel they have lost. Your group depends on interdependence. You risk destroying that relationship and producing lose/lose outcomes if you don't use win/win thinking.

These ground rules are only a few that your team might like to adopt. You need to agree on the importance of ground rules to work together and agree which ground rules to follow. Ground rules must be stated explicitly. Ground rules help define norms, and they allow for process evaluation.

Norms also help new members to adjust their behaviour to fit in with the rest of 'society'. When there is a strong set of ground rules, new team members can more easily integrate themselves into the group. Because they know 'what goes' and what doesn't, their transition is easier and smoother.

Developing your people-process skills

SMTs require a high degree of interdependence. Although you will need technical skills as tasks become more complex, you will find that technical training alone will not ensure your team's success. SMTs seldom fail because members lack technical knowledge. Far more frequently, problems are caused when people can't work together.

SMTs are social systems. Therefore, you will need to focus on your working relationship to ensure success. Sometimes, the more technically orientated members of a SMT will resist interpersonal skills training as being unnecessary. If interpersonal skills are deficient, however, teams will have trouble with conflict resolution, decision-making, self-discipline and communication. When teams lack skills in these areas, they get discouraged and may dump the whole SMT effort. Your team's willingness to participate in people-skills training is a measure of potential success.

Practice may not make perfect

Without training, SMT members are forced to learn interpersonal skills on their own. Although practice 'makes perfect' with some skills, interpersonal and team interaction skills are exceptions. More accurately, *practice with understanding* makes perfect. Without the understanding gained from effective training, people practise their skills incorrectly. Then, unfortunately, *practice makes permanent*, and bad habits are hard to break.

Teams, like individuals, grow into responsibility. Following is a list of growth areas for your team to assess. After each category, determine your level of expertise now, then set a growth goal for yourselves. Goals can include attendance at seminars, feedback sessions, etc. Be sure to set measurable standards, so you can evaluate your progress, then set a realistic date for achieving your goals.

People-process skills assessment

GROUP DECISION-MAKING AND PROBLEM-SOLVING

Group assessment

Today	Future Goal	Standards	Date

CONFRONTATION AND CONFLICT RESOLUTION

Group assessment

Today	Future Goal	Standards	Date

UNDERSTANDING AND WORKING WITH INDIVIDUAL DIFFERENCES

Group assessment

Today	Future Goal	Standards	Date

LISTENING AND FEEDBACK SKILLS

Group assessment

Today	Future Goal	Standards	Date

MANAGING GROUP PROCESS

Group assessment

Today	Future Goal	Standards	Date

EFFECTIVE MEETING MANAGEMENT

Group assessment

Today	Future Goal	Standards	Date

EFFECTIVE PERFORMANCE AND SELF-DISCIPLINE

Group assessment

Today	Future Goal	Standards	Date

Training for people-process skills

You will gain the most from training if you choose for yourselves what training you wish to receive. Also, you should undergo training as a team. You will want to discuss in advance why you want or need a particular kind of training and what should be your team's goals. As you discuss your team's education, you are evaluating your strengths and weaknesses – a form of process evaluation. Defining goals helps to focus your expectations.

When you attend training as a team you increase the transfer of the seminar content to your job setting. Material is presented to all of you in the same way. You can refer to your 'common experience' on the job. Additionally, when you attend training as a team you will usually have a chance to discuss the relevance of the material to your special situation and decide how best to apply the information. Finally, the training experience offers some structured social time for team members to interact without the pressure of day-to-day activities.

You will want to plan for training early in your SMT experience. Early preparation is an investment in the future. 'Pay me now, or pay me later!' is never more true than when thinking about your investment in the critical interpersonal process skills that are vital to the long-term effectiveness of the group.

What skills do you need?

As an individual, you will need certain personal and business-related process skills to be able to participate successfully in an SMT. Listed below are some suggested areas of training you should consider. In which of these skills are you proficient? How proficient are you? Rate yourself by putting an X on the line to show the level of expertise you possess in each area. The results indicate those areas in which you will want to seek additional training.

Problem-solving

Excellent skills   Needs work

├───┤

Managing meetings

Excellent skills   Needs work

├───┤

Decision-making

Excellent skills   Needs work

├───┤

Communication skills

Excellent skills   Needs work

├───┤

Time management

Excellent skills   Needs work

├───┤

General business knowledge

Excellent skills   Needs work

├───┤

Participative management

Excellent skills   Needs work

├───┤

Influencing and being influenced

Excellent skills   Needs work

├───┤

Boundary management

Excellent skills   Needs work

├───┤

Managing office politics

Excellent skills   Needs work

├───┤

Suggestion. You will want to complete as much training as possible while you are on the job. SMT training should be planned and continuous. Work with your team, your internal training professionals, and your SMT sponsor to help you develop your plan.

Review

1. Overall, how would you evaluate your team's facilitative skills?

_____

_____

_____

_____

_____

2. How does your team reach consensus?

_____

_____

_____

_____

_____

3. What is the difference between task ground rules and people-process ground rules?

_____

_____

_____

_____

_____

4. What people-process skills are most important to your team?

_____

_____

_____

_____

_____

_____

CHAPTER 12
Contracting: A Critical Success Factor

Although the establishment of a contract does not guarantee success, operating without one will pretty much guarantee failure.

A team contract is a 'living document'* explicitly outlining team members' agreements with each other in these four key areas: internal management, boundary management, information access and support systems. Your task ground rules should include writing a contract with management. A contract is critical for it lays the groundwork for everything the group does.

Your contract also defines the *roles and responsibilities* within the team and the *ground rules* by which the team will operate. The following pages provide suggestions and sample formats for wording your SMT contract.

The format of a contract will vary from team to team. Typically, however, it begins with a statement such as:

WE, THE UNDERSIGNED, agree to follow the rules
set out to self-manage the _____ group
as of this day, x/x/xx.

Does this wording sound formal? It is! A contract is a formal commitment on the part of the entire team. By making a formal commitment you emphasise the seriousness of your intentions

---

* A living document is a written agreement that you review and update as necessary to meet the group's changing needs. It allows you to benefit from new information based on the group's evolution as an SMT.

both to yourselves and to those who will review and/or approve your contract.

Generally, you will next specify your intentions regarding internal management, boundary management, information access and support systems. Here are some examples of key area contract statements:

The SMT will meet each quarter to establish new objectives, review current team objectives, provide coaching and develop training plans. Individual members will then use the team objectives, as well as their own goals, to establish their own quarterly objectives. The SMT will specify a date when team and individual objectives are to have been achieved.

We agree to perform quarterly peer feedback, using the XYZ Skills Peer Evaluation questionnaire. This input and customer feedback will be used by each individual to prepare his or her annual performance evaluation, which will be subsequently reviewed and approved by the team.

A member of the SMT will attend all SMT staff meetings and share information with the team. Furthermore, each member agrees to share pertinent business information with the SMT in a timely manner, including disseminating information from SMT meetings, budgetary information that affects costs and expenditure, and other informational items deemed relevant.

In addition to the four key areas, individual roles should also be defined and documented within the contract. A role is a prescribed set of duties and/or expected behaviour. It can be permanent or temporary. It can exist independently of a person, that is, it does not always have to be played by the same individual.

In the Vital Link SMT, Philip was originally assigned the role of inducting new members. He had completed new member induction recently himself and knew the most about it. After three months, he turned over the role to Anna, who said she would like to assume that role to improve her facilitating and speaking skills. SMT members often rotate through a set of roles rather than have one member assume a particular role permanently.

Contracting ground rules

Finally, your contract will contain agreement on how you would like to work together. These ground rules spell out expected behaviour of team members on a daily basis. Another term for ground rules is 'group norms', or standards of behaviour. Norms are sometimes spelled out and even made into laws: 'Thou shall not steal.' Other norms are not written but are still expected to be followed, eg, 'Be respectful of your elders.' Regardless of how they are specified, for a group to be successful, ground rules must exist, and they must be followed.

Too often, the ground rules by which a group operates are not made explicit. By making behaviour norms explicit and then creating rules to reinforce them, your team will set expectations early. Team members will know how they are expected to act and interact. Furthermore, you will have time to secure explicit agreement from the group regarding your ground rules.

> When we started our SMT, we said, 'We will never have problems with ground rules. They are so obvious, why waste time discussing them?' The reality was that we had an unexpected problem with people not doing their fair share in our group. We had to go back and establish clear ground rules and it taught us that you can never be too explicit when working in a team.

As with any positive, new relationship, we would like to continue blissfully for ever. If that were always possible, there would be no divorces. As a group, you will find yourselves under tremendous pressure as you work towards your goals. Stress and pressure sabotage human relationships. Without a strong set of ground rules for handling difficult situations, you diminish your chances of recovering successfully from interpersonal problems in your group.

Following are suggestions and work sheets for establishing ground rules in your SMT. Complete the work sheets carefully and use them as guidelines for establishing your operating norms. Be sure to arrive at consensus, then write ground rules into your contract.

1. *Create a common vision of how your group would interact in an ideal situation.* Describe this vision in detail. What would people be doing on a daily basis? How would they behave in meetings? How would they make decisions? Be specific. If someone says, 'We would communicate about the problem', ask '*How* would you communicate and *what* would you say?'

2. *Think of everything that could create interpersonal problems,* eg not doing the job, criticising. Brainstorm together and make a list. Decide on ground rules that the group needs to prevent problems. Following are three examples.

Possible problems	Ground rules
Not doing the job in a responsible way	Talking to the offender and setting standards for how the job is to be done by everyone, every time.
Criticising	Taking the criticism to the team meeting and discussing whether it is warranted or not. If it is, make changes in the way the job is done. If not, ask the critical person to back off.
Arriving late or leaving early	Lateness and leaving early are not permitted unless permission of the team has previously been secured. Reasons must be valid, and everyone must approve.

Listed below are some interpersonal issues to consider. This list will help you to get started on identifying your own issues. Your team should brainstorm as many situations as possible, then write out ground rules for addressing them. Be sure that you achieve consensus on your ground rules from all team members before writing them into your contract.

Possible problems	Ground rules
Making decisions without the team's knowledge	
Not completing tasks on time	
Complaining	
Not participating in team decisions	
Behaviour problems, ie, overcritical behaviour	
Frequently absent from important meetings	

Setting ground rules is just as important as establishing administrative procedures or other 'task-orientated' issues. Ground rules should be written by the group in a spirit of cooperation. Because your contract with its ground rules is a living document, it is not essential to establish all your ground rules at once. As the team works together, other issues or situations will arise that you didn't anticipate. These situations are opportunities for you to review and revise your ground rules as necessary. And it is important to do so!

Contracting: a litmus test

Creating a contract such as the one discussed above is not easy. It is a problem-solving and decision-making task that does not have any 'school solutions'. In other words, the only right answers to problems are ones upon which your team agrees. To

117

complete the task, you will need to share ideas, disagree with each other, modify solutions, and finally agree as a group to a particular solution. Your ability to create a successful contract is directly proportional to your working maturity.

Your working maturity is an accurate predictor of your success in working in a leaderless situation as a self-managing team. If you can establish a contract fairly smoothly, you will have the basic problem-solving and decision-making ability to succeed and win as an SMT.

If your team cannot successfully reach consensus on a contract, you may not be ready to meet the demands of functioning as an SMT. You and your management should reconsider whether self-management is appropriate for your team. While the ability to manage the contracting process successfully does not guarantee your ultimate success, it is a necessary step in the process.

Summary

When you participate in an SMT, you occupy a unique position. You will have more responsibilities and more satisfaction. You will be more things to more people. You may be tempted to spread yourself too thin. Don't be like the little boy who came home from school and said to his mother, 'Sorry I'm late. We were doing a science project at school, and I had to stay and finish the universe.'

To keep yourself on track, review the key principles of this book and set your priorities. To summarise, the key principles include:

Honestly evaluate your personal readiness for an SMT.

Discuss your organisation's commitment to self-management with your team.

Clarify your connection with your sponsor.

Distinguish facts from fables.

Be willing to change.

List your personal and team rewards.

Evaluate your readiness.

Plan your work and work your plan.

Write your contract.

Determine your initial roles.

Recognise political responsibilities.

List action items.

Self-correct as you go.

Develop task-process and people-process ground rules.

Stay flexible.

Evaluate your training needs.

Succeed!

Further Reading from Kogan Page

Building a Dynamic Team, Richard Y Chang, 1995
Building Your Team, Rupert Eales-White, 1995
Healthcare Teams, Peter Mears, 1995
Succeeding as a Self-Managed Team, Richard Y Chang and Mark J Curtin, 1995
Success Through Teamwork, Richard Y Chang, 1995
Team Decision Making Techniques, P Keith Kelly, 1995